# Proving Yourself

## A Study of James

*by Anna Mae Orr*

Aglow. Publications
A Ministry of Women's Aglow Fellowship, Int'l.
P.O. Box I
Lynnwood, WA 98046-1558
USA

# AGLOW BIBLE STUDIES AND WORKBOOKS

## Basic Series

**God's Daughter**
*Practical Aspects of a Christian Woman's Life*

**Basic Beliefs**
*A Primer of Christian Doctrine*

**God's Answer to Overeating**
*A Study of Scriptural Attitudes*

**The Call of Jesus**
*Lessons in Becoming His Disciple*

**Christ in You**
*A Study of the Book of Colossians*

**Triumph Through Temptation**
*How to Conquer Satan's Lies*

**Keys to Contentment**
*A Study of Philippians*

**Drawing Closer to God**
*A Study of Ruth*

**Proving Yourself**
*A Study of James*

**Living by Faith**
*A Study of Romans*

**The Holy Spirit and His Gifts**
*A Study of the Scriptural Gifts*

**Kingdom Living**
*A Study of New Life in Christ*

**Coming Alive in the Spirit**
*The Spirit-Led Life*

**The Quickening Flame**
*A Scriptural Study of Revival*

**A New Commandment**
*Loving As Jesus Loved*

**God's Character**
*A Study of His Attributes*

## Encourager Series

**Restored Value**
*A Woman's Status in Christ*

**Invitation to a Party**
*God's Incredible Hospitality*

## Enrichment Series

**Wholeness From God**
*Patterns and Promises for Health and Healing*

**Teach Us to Pray**
*A Study of the Scriptural Principles of Prayer*

**The Holy Spirit**
*His Person and Purposes*

**The Word**
*God's Manual for Maturity*

**More Than Conquerors**
*The Christian's Spiritual Authority*

**The Beatitudes**
*Expressing the Character of Jesus*

**With Christ in Heavenly Realms**
*A Study of Ephesians*

## Workbook Series

**Introduction to Praise**
*A New Look at the Old Discipline of Praise*

**Time**
*Making It Work for You*

**How to Study the Bible**
*Eight Ways to Better Learn God's Word*

**Spiritual Warfare**
*Strategy for Winning*

**Defense Against Depression**
*The Way to Wholeness*

**Guidance**
*Knowing the Will of God*

*Write for a free catalog.*

# Table of Contents

*Cover design by Ray Braun*

Unless otherwise noted, all Scripture quotations in this publication are from the New American Standard Bible. Other versions are abbreviated as follows: KJV (King James Version), TLB (The Living Bible), TAB (The Amplified Bible).

ISBN 0-930756-75-4

# Introduction

How can I best express my faith and love for Christ? Many Christians continually struggle with this question, especially in confronting the difficult circumstances of life. The Early Church was no different. Most Gentile and Jewish Christians from time to time suffered persecution, lack of material goods and a profound sense of alienation from their society.

The book of *James* was written to Jewish Christians scattered throughout the then known world. Although there is some dispute over its authorship, Bible scholars generally agree that James, "the Lord's brother" (Gal. 1:19), was the writer.

James, who felt it was a higher honor to be called a servant (Jas. 1:1) than to be an apostle or claim a bloodline with Jesus Christ, knew that it is the hard times which bring out the best in Christians. And for this reason he didn't try to soften the impact of the difficulties his readers were facing. Instead, he offered them honest and straightforward answers to their questions. Anyone honestly trying to live the Christian life, anyone looking for practical solutions to daily problems, needs to study this short book.

Because *James* offers such practical advice for us today, at the end of each chapter, you will find questions which summarize the chapter and help you apply the material to your own situations. We suggest that when confronted with the various problems, you use your answers as a checklist to remind you how to react.

Before attempting the study of *James,* we encourage you to read the book through in its entirety at least once. As we study the book of *James,* let us pray that the Holy Spirit will teach us how to "prove ourselves" through our faith in Jesus Christ.

# Proving Yourself in Trials and Temptations

## Introduction

Like many other families in the 1980's, Sue and Tom Barrett were having a hard time making ends meet. When his company was bought out by a national concern, Tom was "let go" from his manager's job. The part-time work he was able to find only provided for the absolute necessities. Although she considered herself a devout Christian, Sue found herself becoming bitter because God was seemingly failing to provide for her family.

All of us have faced difficult circumstances from time to time. The Christians James was writing to certainly were. So, after a quick hello, James goes right to the heart of the problem, which was probably foremost in their mind and which we today still struggle with: What should our response be to the trials and temptations which are part of every person's life?

*Prayer: Dear God, I come humbly to You, knowing that You are the Savior of the world and my personal Savior. Show me how to walk with You through all the trials that enter my life. Let me be confident of victory in You. Lord, open the Scriptures to me this day in an ever new and real way. Amen.*

## Bible Study

Read **James 1:2.**

1. What does James say our attitude should be toward the trials we encounter?

   *one of joy*

In the *New Testament in Modern English,* J.B. Phillips translates this verse, "Don't resent them as intruders, but welcome them as friends." This unexpected advice is echoed by the Apostle Peter in his first epistle.

Read **1 Peter 1:6,7.**

2. What does Peter tell us to do even when we have been distressed by various trials?

*rejoice*

**Discussion Question:** What is our normal reaction when we suffer trials?

To rejoice is our last natural response to hardship. So, in reading these scriptures for the first time, we might be inclined to think that James and Peter had never suffered or else they were "spiritualizing." Neither conclusion is true. Both were later martyred and both were writing to churches under persecution—churches that would see many trials and whose attitude toward those trials would be a crucial factor in their Christian walk.

**Discussion Questions:** Why is attitude so important in facing trials? Why is it so difficult to rejoice in them?

We probably don't normally find joy in hardships because we don't realize how important they are to God. Let's read on and learn the reasons behind this unusual advice.

3. Why does Peter say we have trials?

*to test our faith*

Read **James 1:2-4.**

4. How is endurance produced?

*by the testing of our faith.*

The word which is translated *endurance* here, and as *fortitude* or *patience* in other versions, has no real English equivalent. The Greek word carries the idea of having the ability to turn tragedy into glory. Paul conveyed the same idea in Romans 8:37 when he said, "We are more than conquerors."

5. What synonym for these tests is given in verse 2?

*trials*

This testing or proving of our faith by the trials we experience is one of the most important ideas expressed in the Bible. Why do we have trials and tribulations in this life? Both Peter and James would strongly assert: *to test or prove our faith.*

**Discussion Question:** Share how a trial in your life has served to test your faith.

Reread **1 Peter 1:6,7.**
6.  How important is this testing of our faith to God?

_____

7.  How may our faith be tested?

_____

**Discussion Question:** Why do you think it is necessary for God to test our faith?

Fire, in the Bible, is frequently an instrument of cleansing. By the use of fire, God examines us to find out what we may have that is "stubble," unnecessary, unclean or unholy.

**Discussion Questions:** In what countries is the Church being persecuted today? Do you think James and Peter would give the same advice to the Christians there?

If we stop and think about it, we realize how much comfort this concept can give us. Not only have God's people always wondered how to face trials, but also why. Deep down inside we want to know that there is a reason for whatever we are enduring and that it is not just some chance circumstance. The fact that we _know_ there is a purpose in everything that happens to us gives us a profound assurance that the God of Creation is also the God in charge of our lives and that something will truly be accomplished by whatever is taking place.

8.  The idea of God's testing man is also a familiar one in the Old Testament. Beside each scripture reference, write the instrument God used and the purpose of the testing in each case.

|  | **Instrument** | **Purpose** |
|---|---|---|
| Ex. 16:4 | | |
| | | |
| Ex. 20:18,19 | | |
| | | |
| Deut. 8:2 | | |
| | | |

Judg. 2:21,22 _____

_____

2 Chron. 32:31 _____

_____

9.  Summarize the reason(s) why God tests our faith.

_____

_____

_____

Throughout our Christian walk we are going to find ourselves periodically tested. Although the writers of the Bible may express their ideas in slightly different ways, the same idea is evident: *God tests us to know what is in our heart, to see if our faith is strong enough to make us obedient to Him so that we will not sin.*

Although Paul, the Apostle to the Gentiles, did not refer to the sufferings he endured for the Lord's sake as trials, he expressed much the same attitude toward them.

**Read Romans 5:3.**
10.  How does Paul describe his attitude toward his tribulations?

_____

**Read 2 Corinthians 1:3-5.**
11.  How does he describe his afflictions?

_____

**Discussion Question:** What are some of these "momentary and light" afflictions Paul suffered? (If you aren't sure, read 2 Corinthians 11:23-29.)

**Discussion Question:** How can we reconcile the so-called "prosperity doctrine" that says Christians should never suffer, never know poverty or other unpleasantnesses in life, with this teaching?

Of course, you can't reconcile these two doctrines. The Bible does not teach that the Christian will never suffer. Rather, it teaches that the testing of our faith is so important to God it may even be tested by fire.

These letters were not written to frighten Christians, but rather to give us an understanding of what we may have to experience in our life.

12. What great promise do we have in these verses?

_____

13. Why?

_____

_____

**Discussion Question:** Can you share a time when someone else who has gone through a similar experience has comforted you in a time of affliction?

Read **Hebrews 13:5,6.**

14. What precious promise do we have from Christ?

_____

15. What should we confidently say?

_____

God never promised us a rose garden, a life free from problems, trouble or trials. What He did promise us is that we need never go through such experiences alone? No matter what hard experiences we go through, Jesus Christ our Lord and Savior has promised to go through them with us.

**Discussion Question:** Can you describe a "hard" time which Jesus walked through with you?

Read **1 Corinthians 10:13.**
16. What additional promises concerning problem times are we given?

_____

_____

_____

These are good and wonderful promises from the Lord that we must remember and rely on during our times of testings.

**Discussion Question:** Relate a testing time and the way of escape God provided.

One other fact should give us hope. The two main words that are translated *trial, temptation,* etc., in the New Testament contain in them the idea of a test we are expected to pass, and trials that are for our good. That should excite us. We need to develop the point of view that a time of testing is not a time for grumbling and complaining, but a time of expectation. We need to look at tests as experiences we are ready to pass, and also as experiences that are going to help develop some quality of character in us that God wants developed.

17. Beside each scripture reference, put the characteristics to be developed or the reward to be gained.

Romans 5:3 _____

James 1:12 _____

James 1:2-4 _____

_____

1 Peter 1:6,7 _____

_____

1 Peter 4:12-16 _____

_____

We need to clear up one important point regarding our thinking and some teaching about periods of trial. We acknowledge the fact that with every trial there is the possibility of failure; there is also the temptation to blame God and to do wrong—sin, commit evil. Sinful man has usually blamed God when he has felt tempted to commit evil. Is this a fair charge?

Read **James 1:13-15.**
18. What should no one ever say?

_____

10

19.  Why?

_____

Although the words are not actually there, the intent of this idea is that God does not tempt anyone to commit evil.

20.  How is a person tempted then?

_____

The word *lust* as James used it simply meant a strong desire.

21.  Fill in these blank spaces.

When lust_____it_____,

and when sin_____,

it brings forth_____.

### Read **Mark 7:21.**
22.  What does Jesus say comes out of the human heart?

_____

_____

_____

_____

**Personal Question:** Which sins on this list do you find in your heart?

It's easy for Christians to try to rationalize sin and believe that because they don't commit murder or adultery, they are all right. But we need to realize that God places importance on all other sins as well and to remind ourselves that He doesn't have a "rating system" in which one sin is worse than another. The human heart is deceitful and we must recognize that fact so that we can constantly contend against it.

### Read **Matthew 4:3.**
23.  What is Satan called in this verse?

_____

No, God never tempts man to do evil. Rather it is that interplay between Satan, the tempter, and the desires of the human heart that causes us to do wrong and to fail the various trials and tests that come to us.

Reread **James 1:14,15.**
24.    List the six steps in temptation.

_____

_____

**Personal Questions:** List each of these six steps on a piece of paper. Choose an occasion when you were tempted and sinned. Beside each step, write the steps of your personal temptation. At what point did the temptation become sin? What might you have done to have stopped the process?

Read **Romans 6:23.**
25.    The wages of sin is death, but what is the gift of God?

_____

The joyful Christian in the face of testing and trials is a powerful witness to an unhappy, defeated world. No one will dispute that, but how do we develop this attitude of joy? Does the Bible give us any help along this line?

Read **Romans 8:6.**
26.    How does the Apostle Paul say we can achieve life and peace?

_____

Read **1 Peter 4:16.**
27.    What does Peter urge the person who is reviled as a Christian to do?

_____

Read **2 Corinthians 4:17,18.**
28.    How does Paul tell us to understand this "momentary light affliction?"

_____

This is powerful advice if we will only follow it. During times of testing we must take our eyes off our circumstances and turn them to God, praising and worshiping Him. In place of self-pity, we must develop the attitude of joyful expectancy toward the future and what God has planned for us.

Reread **James 1:2-4.**
29. What is the final result of the endurance we develop through trials?

_____

There are two Greek words which are translated *perfect* in English. The first is the glorified state which is obtained when we receive our glorified bodies for eternity. The other, and this is the meaning here, is a mature, thoroughly instructed, deeply experienced lifestyle.

**Personal Application**
Write down one or more trials you are personally going through. What is your attitude toward this testing? Do you need to change it? What qualities do you think God wants to change or form in you? What are you going to do to cooperate with Him?

**Memory Work**
*"Consider it all joy, my brethren, when you encounter various trials, knowing that the testing of your faith produces endurance. And let endurance have its perfect result, that you may be perfect and complete, lacking in nothing"* (Jas. 1:2-4).

## PROVING YOURSELF IN TRIALS
When you are being tempted or tried,
1. What are the steps which will turn this trial or temptation into sin?
2. What will you do to keep yourself from sinning?
3. Why are you being tested? (If you don't know, list some of the possibilities?
4. What attitude will you have?
5. How will you develop and maintain this attitude?
6. What may God be trying to accomplish through this time of testing?
7. What is the final result of this trial?

## Lesson Two

# Proving Yourself in Prayer

## Introduction

For several years Carol had been praying that her mother-in-law would be saved. Yet, it was as though her prayers were completely ignored by God.

The older woman showed as little interest in spiritual things as she ever had, and, in fact, seemed increasingly hostile to Carol's attempts to talk to her about God. Lately, Carol found herself losing faith in her ability to pray at all.

There are few of us who haven't struggled with the question of why so many prayers seem to go unanswered. James addresses himself to this question and also provides us with clues to help us improve the quality of our prayer life.

*Prayer: Heavenly Father, guide me in the study of Your Word through the power of the Holy Spirit. Help me to search for You with my whole heart so that I may better hear what You are saying to me. Forgive me for the times I have failed to put You first in my life. In Jesus' name. Amen.*

## Bible Study

Read **James 1:5.**
1. What is James' counsel when we don't know what to do in a given situation?

_____

Later on in the book of *James,* the author re-emphasizes the importance of going to God with our needs.

Read **James 4:2.**
2. What does James say is the cause of much of the lack in our life?

_____

Too often, when we have a need, we do everything we can humanly think of and turn to God as a last resort. If we would ask God as a first

14

step, we would save ourselves a lot of problems.

**Personal Question:** List what you need that you have not asked God for.

**Discussion Question:** Why do we wait so long to ask God for help?

The fact that we choose to try to solve our own problems before asking God seems to indicate a basic lack of trust on our part. For some reason we believe that we can handle our problems better than God can.

**Read James 1:6-8.**
3.   When we go to God with a need, how should we ask?

_____

This is the key to receiving from God. We must come to Him with the sure confidence that He will answer our prayer, giving us what we need.

4.   Describe the person who doubts.

_____

_____

5.   Who cannot expect to receive anything from the Lord?

_____

6.   What is a synonym for double-minded?

_____

**Personal Question:** List any areas in your life about which you are double-minded.

A double-minded or unstable person has no settled principles and is controlled by his emotions. His spiritual life suffers because of the instability of his commitment to God. Although the Bible uses different images, it has more to say about the spiritual difficulties faced by such a person.

**Read Luke 16:13.**
7.   Why did Jesus say it is impossible to serve two masters?

_____

**Discussion Question:** Why do you think this is so?

Many of us try to serve two masters in this life? God and our job. God and our good times. God and money. Although it may seem possible to do this for a time, there will come a day when the two "masters" will come into strong conflict and we will be faced to make a choice.

**Read 1 Corinthians 10:21.**
8.  What is Paul's example of this kind of double-mindedness?

_____

_____


**Read Luke 9:62.**
9.  What does Jesus say about someone who is double-minded (looks back)?

_____


This is a strong indictment. Yet, who can deny the truth of Jesus' words!

**Discussion Question:** Can you share a situation in which you were double-minded and the results?

This same idea is reflected in the Lord's rebuke to the Church in Laodicea.

**Read Revelation 3:14-16.**
10.  Of what does the Lord accuse the Laodiceans?

_____


11.  What does He say He will do?

_____


**Read Ephesians 4:14.**
12.  Describe the faith of an immature person.

_____

_____

_____

There is a remarkable similarity between Paul's description of a "baby Christian" and James' description of a double-minded person.

13.  If we compare these two verses of scripture we might go so far as

to say that a double-minded person is _____
in faith.

The Christian walk demands wholeheartedness in our commitment to Christ and His kingdom.

**Discussion Question:** If there are areas of our life in which we are double-minded, what should we do? (James 1:5, 6 may help.)

Double-mindedness and lack of faith, however, are only two reasons why our prayers seem to go unanswered. Scripture points out others.
14.  Write the reason given in the space following each scripture.

Deut. 1:43-46  _____

Ps. 66:18  _____

Prov. 1:28,29  _____

_____

Prov. 21:13  _____

_____

Prov. 28:9  _____

Isa. 1:15  _____

Isa. 59:2; Micah 3:4_____

Zech. 7:12,13  _____

James 4:3  _____

**Personal Questions:** Has God revealed to you one or more reasons from this list why your prayers are not being answered? If so, what should you do about this?

Sin is probably the most common reason that our prayers are not answered. But there are others, which the Christian must know about so she will not suffer false condemnation; and will be more effective in prayer.

Read **2 Corinthians 12:7-11.**

15. What was Paul's prayer?

_____

16. What was God's answer?

_____

_____

17. Did God do what Paul wanted?

_____

18. What was Paul's response?

_____

_____

_____

19. What does Paul say was God's reason for saying no?

_____

God knew that the temptation for Paul to be lifted up in pride might be too great and so He did not answer Paul's prayer the way Paul had hoped.

Although Paul might have been tempted to sin and to blame God for not taking care of this problem for him, he accepted God's answer with a gracious spirit and turned this trial into a victory.

Read **Daniel 10:12,13.**

20. Why did the angel come to Daniel?

_____

21. Why was the angel delayed?

_____

_____

Occasionally, at least, answers to our prayers are delayed by spiritual events we know nothing of. Like Daniel, we need to persevere in our prayers until we see the answer.

When we seem not to have an answer to our prayers, we need to ask God if there _is_ sin or double-mindedness which may be hindering the answer. If we ask honestly, we know that God will tell us if this is the

18

reason that we have no answer. If He does not, then we should continue to pray until the answer is received or He tells us why the delay.

Let's take a look now at the other side of the coin—who is the person who receives answers to his prayers.

Read **Mark 9:23.**
22. To whom are all things possible?

_____

Read **1 John 5:14.**
23. What confidence do we have in God?

_____

Read **John 14:13.**
24. Why will God do anything asked in Jesus' name?

_____

To receive answers to our prayers, we must make up our minds to "will with God one will" and believe that He will do what Scripture says He will do.

Read **John 15:7.**
25. When can we ask God for whatever we wish?

_____

The Amplified Bible translates this verse as "If you live in Me—abide vitally united to me—and My words remain in you and continue to live in your hearts, ask what you will and it shall be done for you."

**Discussion Question:** What does abiding in the Lord mean to you?

The word _abide_ implies a long-lasting or permanent dwelling. There is nothing transient or short-lived about an abiding relationship. It is for keeps.

Read **John 16:24.**
26. Why does God give us what we ask for?

_____

Does it surprise you that God desires joy for us. It shouldn't. God wants us to be full of joy. Joy is one of the fruits of the Spirit. When others see joy in us, they are more likely to be attracted to the Lord.

**Discussion Question:** What is the purpose of prayer?

Christian prayer should never be an attempt to change the mind of God, for He already wants the best for us. Christian prayer is the opening of the heart to the transforming influence of the Spirit of God.

The book of *James* shares further insights which can aid us in our prayer life.

Read **James 5:13,14.**

27. When does James say we should pray?

28. What should we do when we are sick?

When one is sick, if it is possible, the afflicted should call the spiritual leaders and not wait for them to learn about the need from other sources.

29. What are the elders to do in addition to praying for the sick?

Read **Luke 10:34.**

30. What did the Good Samaritan do to the wounds of the injured man?

It was customary among the Jews to carry oil with them on all journeys to anoint their bodies and heal their wounds and bruises. Anointing with oil was a First Century remedy for many types of injuries. Today, it is a symbol of God's healing by the power of the Holy Spirit.

**Discussion Question:** Describe a time you or someone you know was healed.

Read **James 5:15,16.**

31. What will restore the one who is sick?

32.  Who raises up the sick?

_____

33.  If the illness is caused by sin, what should the person do?

_____

Confession should always be made first to God and then to anyone we may have wronged. If we are sick and are conscious that we have injured any person, we need to make the confession to him. Those who have done injury and those who are injured should, if possible, pray together for each other.

34.  The success of the prayer does not depend on talent, education

or office but on _____

Read **Mark 2:5.**
35.  How did Jesus heal the sick man of palsy?

_____

_____

Read **James 5:17,18.**
36.  What prayer of Elijah's is referred to here?

_____

_____

_____

37.  What does James say about Elijah (v. 17)?

_____

**Discussion Question:** Read 1 Kings 17:1; 18:1, 42-45 and Luke 4:25. In what ways do you think Elijah was like us?

In saying that Elijah was "a man with a nature like ours," James seems to be saying we should be seeing the same kind of miraculous answers to prayers that Elijah did.

**Discussion Questions:** How do you feel about this idea? Have you accepted the possible power of your prayers? Why?

**Personal Application:**
This coming week I plan to improve my prayer life by

1. _____

2. _____

3. _____

## Memory Work
*"Therefore, confess your sins to one another, and pray for one another, so that you may be healed. The effective prayer of a righteous man can accomplish much" (Jas. 5:16).*

## PROVING YOURSELF IN PRAYER
1. What is the first thing to do when you have a need?
2. What attitude will you have as you pray?
3. If you have trouble having this attitude, what should you do?
4. List reasons prayers are not always answered.
5. If your prayer seems to go unanswered, what will you do?
6. Why does God answer prayer?
7. What assurance does this give you?
8. How much power does your prayer have?

# Proving Yourself in Wisdom

## Introduction

Eve began man's age old search for wisdom, when in open disobedience, she ate fruit from the forbidden tree of the knowledge of good and evil. Like her, man has, however, mistaken *knowing* for wisdom. And, like her, man has always believed that he can gain wisdom through his own efforts—by studying scholarly books, thinking and searching for solutions. But the wisdom of God is primarily the wisdom to rightly handle *all* of God's gifts to us. Because James knew that the churches he was writing to were troubled by the claims of self-appointed teachers who boasted of their knowledge, he set guidelines which would enable them to distinguish the wisdom of God from man's wisdom.

*Prayer: Heavenly Father, I greatly need Your wisdom. Please guide me through the study of Your Word, and show me how to apply Your wisdom in my life. In Jesus' name. Amen.*

**Discussion Question:** What modern parallels do we find to the situation James found in the Early Church?

**Discussion Questions:** What is the difference between knowledge and wisdom? How would you characterize man's wisdom as opposed to God's?

## Bible Study

Read **James 1:5.**
1.  James says if we lack wisdom we should_____

**Discussion Question:** For what reasons or situations might we need to ask for God's wisdom?

2.  To whom does God give wisdom and how does He give it?

_____

Not only does God give us the wisdom we request, He gives it to us generously and without being critical of our need to ask Him.

Read **2 Chronicles 1:9-12.**
3. When Solomon was made king, what was his prayer?

_____

_____

4. What was God's response?

_____

_____

At this point in history, Solomon's heart was right with God, and, instead of asking selfishly, he asked for gifts that would enable him to rule well. God was so pleased with his request, He gave Solomon all the treasures other kings might have asked for.

**Discussion Question:** If God made the same offer to you that He made to Solomon, what would you ask for?

Sadly, Solomon did not follow God's wisdom all of his life, and, consequently, the glory and honor with which God blessed his kingdom departed with his death.

Read **Genesis 3:1-6.**

From the very beginning, man has always placed a high value on wisdom. Unfortunately, he has not always looked for the right kind of wisdom, nor has he gone about finding it in the right way.

5. Why did Eve succumb to Satan's tempting?

_____

Read **Ecclesiastes 1:18.**
6. What does the writer of Ecclesiastes tell us about man's wisdom and knowledge?

_____

We have only to look at the history of the world to recognize the truth of this statement. Man, acting on his own wisdom, has come close to destroying himself and his world on more than one occasion.

Read **Jeremiah 9:23,24.**

24

7. Instead of a man boasting in his wisdom, what does Jeremiah say someone should boast about?

_____

Read **James 3:13-16.**
8. What are some of the characteristics of man's wisdom?

_____

_____

9. How does James describe such wisdom?

_____

Read **Isaiah 29:14.**
10. What happens to man's wisdom?

_____

Read **1 Corinthians 1:18-25.**
11. What is God doing to do with this kind of wisdom (v. 19)?

_____

Man's wisdom and God's wisdom are diametrically opposed to each other.

12. How does God's wisdom compare to man's?

_____

Perhaps we have not always recognized God's wisdom when He has given it to us because it seemed like "foolishness" to us.

**Discussion Question:** Discuss some of the examples given in the Bible when God's "foolishness' triumphed over man's wisdom.

Read **Isaiah 33:5,6.**
13. How is the Messiah described in these verses?

_____

_____

Read **Isaiah 11:1,2.**

25

14. What characteristics are given here?

_____

_____

_____

Wisdom is one of the characteristics of God, and when Jesus returns for the second time, the whole earth will be aware of His wisdom.

Read **James 3:17.**
15. How does James describe God's wisdom?

_____

_____

_____

James' description of God's wisdom provides a yardstick against which we can measure our wisdom.

**Discussion Question:** Most of us know what we must do to acquire human knowledge, but how can we be sure of obtaining God's wisdom?

Read **Proverbs 3:5,6.**
16. What do these verses tell us we must do to gain wisdom and have God direct our paths?

_____

_____

**Discussion Question:** Can you share a time when you trusted God, rather than your understanding of a situation and what happened?

Read **Proverbs 9:10.**
17. What is the beginning of wisdom?

_____

Read **Micah 6:9.**

26

18.  How is wisdom described in these two verses?

_____

The *fear of the Lord* is an expression used often by Biblical writers. Rather than being the kind of fear we understand the word to mean today, it means *reverential trust,* including the hatred of evil.

Read **Proverbs 4:5,7.**
19.  What are we commanded to acquire_____

The Living Bible paraphrases Proverbs 4:7: "Determination to be wise is the first step toward becoming wise."

**Personal Question:** In your heart are you really determined to be wise

and to do what is required to be wise?_____If your answer to this question is *no,* you probably will never have wisdom.

Read **Job 28:28.**
20.  How does this verse in Job define understanding?

_____

21.  Read the following scriptures and list the rewards of finding God's wisdom.

Prov. 3:16_____

Prov. 3:17_____

Prov. 3:18_____

Prov.  3:21,22_____

Prov. 3:23_____

Prov. 3:24_____

Prov. 4:6 _____

Prov. 4:8 _____

Prov. 4:9 _____

_____

22. Beside the following scriptures, write the value placed on wisdom.

Proverbs 3:13_____

Proverbs 3:14_____

Proverbs 3:15_____

_____

Proverbs 3:16_____

Proverbs 3:18_____

Read **James 3:13.**
23. How does a person show he is wise?

_____

Jesus said much the same thing in the Gospel of Matthew.

Read **Matthew 11:19.**
24. What is wisdom vindicated by?

_____

Read **Matthew 7:24.**
25. What does Jesus say a wise man does?

_____

Wisdom isn't just knowledge to be stored in the head. It is to be acted on.

**Discussion Question:** What specific kinds of actions are motivated by Godly wisdom.

Read **2 Timothy 3:15.**
26. The Bible is able to give us wisdom that leads to_____

_____

Since the wisdom of God is often foolishness to man, we may appear unwise to our family and friends. However, God's wisdom always proves to be the right direction to follow.

**Discussion Question:** Can you share an experience in which you appeared foolish at the time, but in the end you knew that it was God's wisdom which had directed you?

Read **1 Corinthians 12:4-11.**
There is still one aspect of wisdom we have not looked at.

27. List the gifts of the Spirit.

_____

_____

_____

The gift of the word of wisdom spoken of here is supernatural wisdom given to the Spirit-filled believer for a specific situation and time.

Read **1 Corinthians 1:24.**
28. Who is the wisdom of God?

_____

**Personal Application**
How have you approached the need for wisdom? By trying to get it for yourself, or by asking God for it? How will you apply what you learned in this chapter to a particular situation in your life right now?

**Memory Work**
*"But if any of you lacks wisdom, let him ask of God, who gives to all men generously and without reproach, and it will be given to him. But let him ask in faith without any doubting, for the one who doubts is like the surf of the sea driven and tossed by the wind" (Jas. 1:5,6).*

## PROVING YOURSELF IN WISDOM
1. List at least three ways we get godly wisdom.
2. Why do we need God's wisdom?
3. Man's wisdom is characterized by
4. God's wisdom is characterized by
5. What are the results or rewards of godly wisdom?
6. What should we do with godly wisdom?

# Proving Yourself with Riches

## Introduction

How should I handle my money?

The Christian life and the life lived in step with the world are in sharp contrast. And there is no place where the contrast is sharper than in the two viewpoints about wealth and the power it brings. James helps us come to a healthy understanding of money by showing its importance in the context of eternity.

*Prayer: Heavenly Father, I pray for Your guidance and understanding in studying Your Holy Word. Show me the proper place of material possessions in my life, and in the life of my fellowship. In Jesus' name. Amen.*

**Discussion Question:** What should the Christian's attitude toward money be?

## Bible Study

Read **James 1:9-11.**

1. According to James what should the brother of humble circumstances glory in?

_____

2. The rich man glory in his _____
3. Why is the rich man compared with flowering grass?

_____

Grass is herbage in general, including flowers. At times in Palestine a hot southeasterly wind called *sirocco* comes sweeping across the land. This wind can change the color of the landscape from green to brown in a single day.

4. What is the end result of the rich man according to James?

_____

The translation of these verses in *The Amplified Bible* helps us to better understand what James is saying: "Let the brother in humble circumstances glory in his elevation [as a Christian, called to the true riches and to be an heir of God]; and the rich [person ought to glory] in being humbled [by being shown his human frailty] because like the flower of the grass he will pass away."

It should not be implied from the above verses that James was condemning wealth in general; rather, he was condemning the evil practices that are frequently associated with its acquisition and the power it generates.

He was also very much aware of a related problem caused by our human nature.

Read **James 2:1-4.**
5.   Of what attitude was James critical?

_____

The Greek word from which this expression is taken means to estimate people superficially rather than on the basis of their fundamental humanity. In a Christian fellowship there is no room for prejudice or playing favorites. When the church first started, everything was shared in common, but human nature soon took over, and partiality toward the wealthy was soon displayed.

6.   How was this favoritism being exhibited in the churches James addressed?

_____

_____

_____
7.   How does James describe anyone who displays favoritism?

_____

_Favoritism_ and its opposite, _prejudice,_ have been a blight on every society. There is something in our human nature that causes us to make distinctions, even among Christians, favoring some and rejecting others. This is completely against Christ's teachings.

**Personal Question:** Ask the Lord to bring to mind some of your prejudices that hurt Him. Then confess them, ask His forgiveness and determine to put them aside.

Read **James 2:5-9.**

8. What is the contrast James gives between the poor and the rich?

_____

_____

_____

_____

**Discussion Question:** Why are the poor so chosen of God?

9. When we show partiality what are we doing?

_____

The sin of partiality is not limited to the rich. It is one we can all be guilty of. James' indictment against the wicked wealthy is particularly strong.

Read **James 5:1-6.**
10. What "crimes" does James accuse the wealthy of committing?

_____

_____

_____

_____

11. What judgments await those who do these things?

_____

_____

_____

_____

During His ministry on earth, Jesus, too, warned of the love of money.

Read **Luke 18:18-27.**

This is the familiar story of the rich, young ruler who asked Jesus what he must do to inherit eternal life.

12. What was Jesus' first response?


13. When the young man said he had kept them all, what did Jesus say?

_____

_____

14. How did the young man respond to Jesus' words?

_____

15. What was Jesus' comment?

_____

_____


**Personal Questions:** Does Jesus' statement bother you at all? If so, why do you think this is so?

**Discussion Questions:** In telling the rich young man to sell everything he had, is Jesus demanding this of everyone? If not, why not?

The rich young man's sin was not that he was wealthy, but that he loved his wealth more than he loved the Lord.

**Personal Questions:** Is there anything presently in your life that you love more than the Lord? Are you willing to give it up? If so, tell the Lord right now.

Although there are many gods or idols that we may be tempted to hold above our love of God, wealth seems to hold special temptations.

**Read 1 Timothy 6:10.**
16. According to Paul's letter to Timothy, what does he call the love of money?

_____

17. What has happened to some who have longed for money?

_____

_____


The Early Church had been given a dramatic example of what can hap-

33

pen when someone loves money too much.

Read **Acts 5:1-11.**
18. Give a brief summary of the event related here.


We are prone to forget that when God came to earth, He chose a poor (by the world's standards) family in an obscure village in which to be born. In both the Old and the New Testaments, God has always shown a special love for the poor.

Read **Luke 4:14-18.**
19. When Jesus announced His ministry, what four groups did He mention?

_____

20. What provisions for the poor did God make in the following scriptures?

Ex. 22:25_____

Lev. 19:10_____

Deut. 15:1-4_____

Ps. 69:33 _____

Gal. 2:10 _____

21. What was to be the fate of those who were unkind to the poor?

Prov. 21:13_____

Prov. 22:16_____

Prov. 22:23_____

Prov. 28:9 _____

Read **Ezekiel 22:29.**
22. What were some of God's complaints against Israel before the captivity?

_____

_____

23. List some of the rewards of those who take care of the poor.

Proverbs 14:21_____

Proverbs 19:17_____

Proverbs 22:9 _____

Proverbs 28:27_____

God's original plan for His people included provisions to take care of gross inequalities of wealth.

Read **Leviticus 25:10-17.**
24. What was the year of Jubilee?

_____

25. What happened during that year?

_____

Read **Leviticus 25:23-28.**
26. What happened to land that had been "sold"?

_____

_____

Read **Leviticus 25:39-41.**
27. What was the law regarding a poor Israelite who had sold himself for service?

_____

_____

In other words, every 50 years after the Israelites had come into the Promised Land, they were to begin all over again. (Incidentally, there is no record that they ever were obedient to this law.)

**Discussion Questions:** Would you like your government to adopt such a law? Why or why not?

The practice of tithing was another safeguard God used to bring constantly to remembrance that He was the source of all, and as a way to regulate the effects of greed. Someone has estimated that all the tithes and offerings God demanded of the Jews amounted to approximately 30% of their income.

Christians are not bound by the tithe, but by an acknowledgment that *everything* belongs to God. This does not free us from giving to the work of the Church, but gives us the liberty to give much beyond the 10% tithe. Giving truly begins where tithing ends.

**Personal Questions:** What is your standard of giving? On what is it based? Would you want God to give to you according to the standard you give to Him?

Read **Matthew 6:19-21.**
28. In your own words write out the relationship Jesus expressed between love and money/possessions?

_____

_____

**Personal Question:** Honestly, what do you love most in your life?

29. What is one possible reason Jesus tells us to store up our treasure in heaven?

_____

Read **Matthew 6:30-33.**
30. What secret did Jesus give us so we do not have to worry about finances?

_____

_____

**Personal Question:** What does your use of the wealth God has given you reflect about your personal priorities?

**Personal Questions:** Can you truly say that seeking God's kingdom and His righteousness has top priority in your life? If not, what are you going to do about it?

Read **Luke 18:28-30.**
31. What did Jesus say will be given to those who give up their homes and families (make themselves poor) for His sake?

_____

_____

_____

_____

**Personal Application**
1.  Review your use of money over the past year. Approximately how
    much did you spend on
    Food
    Clothing
    Housing
    God
    Personal and family recreation
    Extras
2.  What priorities does your spending reflect?
3.  List ways that you can make any necessary changes.

**Memory Work**
*"Listen, my beloved brethren: did not God choose the poor of this world
to be rich in faith and heirs of the kingdom which He promised to those
who love Him?" (Jas. 2:5).*
*"For the love of money is a root of all sorts of evil, and some by long-
ing for it have wandered away from the faith, and pierced themselves
with many a pang" (1 Tim. 6:10).*

## PROVING YOURSELF IN RICHES
1.  God's view of money is...
2.  List the advantages the poor have.
3.  List the disadvantages the rich have.
4.  Do you believe this? How does your lifestyle reflect what
    you believe?
5.  How much of what you have belongs to God?
6.  The secret to establishing your priorities is...

# Proving Yourself in Self-Control and Obedience

## Introduction

Mary constantly seemed to be on a diet. As hard as she tried, she never lost much weight permanently. Irregular eating habits were a way of life with her. Often when she was in a hurry, she didn't take time to eat regular meals but snacked throughout the day. At bedtime, she usually ate a dish of ice cream, promising herself that she wouldn't eat breakfast. Mary couldn't understand why her weight remained such a problem.

James reminds us that the Word of God acts as a mirror enabling us to see our own defects and shortcomings. Only through the power of the Holy Spirit can we learn the self-control and obedience needed to begin to reflect the life of Christ.

*Prayer: Heavenly Father, open my mind and my heart to Your direction for my life. Help me to be willing to obey and follow Your plan for my life instead of my own. In Jesus' name. Amen.*

**Discussion Question:** Why is self-control so important for the Christian to develop?

## Bible Study

Read **James 1:16, 17.**
1.   Where does every good gift originate?

_____

Light is a symbol of both knowledge and purity. God, the Father of lights, is compared to the sun which rises and sets each day as the seasons change. However with God there is no varying or changing, no shadow of turning.

Read **Hebrews 13:8.**
2.   How does *Hebrews* express this same idea of the changelessness of God?

_____

**Discussion Questions:** Can you truly accept this fact of Jesus Christ—that He never changes—that He is the same Jesus as described in the Gospels? What exceptions have you made?

Read **1 John 1:5.**
3.  Compare light and darkness with God.

_____

Read **James 1:18.**
4.  How does God bring forth mankind?

_____

The Amplified Bible says that "He gave us birth (as sons)..." This is a spiritual birth.

Read **1 Corinthians 15:20-23.**
5.  What is Christ called in this passage?

_____

6.  Adam brought death, what did Christ bring?

_____

Christ is the first fruit of the grave. He, by His resurrection overcame death.

7.  Who else is promised a resurrection?

_____

Reread **James 1:18.**
8.  According to James, who were the first fruits among God's creatures?

_____

To understand the significance of the first fruits, we need to go back to the Old Testament. The Feast of the Harvest of the First Fruits of the Israelites' labor was one of three national feasts celebrated each year. For that occasion, God commanded His people to "Bring the choice of first fruits of your soil into the house of the Lord your God" (Ex. 23:19). These first fruits, which gave promises of the coming harvest, were dedicated to God.

**Discussion Question:** What are our first fruits today?

**Personal Question:** Do you always remember to give God your first fruits?

Here, we see the Christian in two aspects: first, she is herself a kind of first fruit, designed to be the special possession of God, the pledge and earnest of a redeemed race; second, we are also worshipers, who come offering the first fruits of our labors to God.

Read **James 1:19,20.**
9. What behavior does James urge upon us?

_____

_____

10. What doesn't achieve the righteousness of God?

_____

Man in his natural state is a creature of extremes and excesses. No place is this more obvious or dangerous than with our temper. Lack of control in this area has been one of man's problems since the beginning of the human race.

Read **Genesis 4:3-8.**
11. What was Cain's reaction when God regarded Abel's offering favorably but not his?

_____

12. What was the result of his anger?

_____

We see this same seed of anger in Cain's descendants.

Read **Genesis 4:19-24.**
13. What reasons did Lamech give for killing?

_____

In our natural condition, any slight or offense becomes a cause for anger and even more.

Read **Proverbs 15:18 and 22:24.**
14. The Bible has much to say about anger. What does it say in these two references?

_____

Read **Ephesians 4:26,31.**
15. What instructions does Paul give the Ephesians concerning anger?

_____

_____

_____

Read **Titus 1:7.**
16. What does Paul say an overseer should not be?

_____

_____

Read **Proverbs 16:32.**
17. Who are considered better than the mighty?

_____

The righteousness of God becomes the right conduct that God calls us to. The anger of man does not work the righteousness of God because it is usually evoked by a clash of wills, a conflict of selfish interests, a struggle for power.

**Discussion Question:** What steps can we take to control our temper, thereby becoming slow to anger?

Read **Psalms 103:8 and 145:8.**
18. What qualities of God are given in these psalms?

_____

God's nature stands in stark contrast to that of natural man.

James now turns his attention to another subject—obedience.

Read **James 1:21.**
19. What does James tell us to put aside?

_____

A corrupt mind full of sensuality and wickedness is not favorable to the reception of the truth.

20.  According to James 1:21 what is able to save our souls?

_____

21.  How should the Word implanted be received?

_____

_____

We should allow the principles of the Gospel to become implanted in our own nature. By this implanting, regardless of how bad our fruits have been in the past, the implanted Word will produce fruits of righteousness in our lives.

**Discussion Questions:** Share how the principles of the Gospel have become a reality in your life. When did the Word of God become implanted in your innermost being?

Read **James 1:22-25.**
22.  What is the test of true obedience?

_____

We deceive ourselves as to our spiritual state by the enjoyment of religious discussions, fluency of speech on religious themes, passion in religious disputes or diligence in performance of religious ceremonies. However, only when we act upon the Word of God, do we prove that we believe it.

Read **1 John 2:17.**
23.  Who does John tell us will abide forever?

_____

Read **Romans 2:13.**
24.  Who will be justified before God?

_____

Read **Matthew 12:50.**
25.  Who does Jesus consider His brother and sister and mother?

_____

Read **James 1:24,25.**
26.  What does a man do after he looks at his natural face in a mirror?

_____

An ordinary mirror tells us little or nothing about ourselves, but in looking in the Word of God, which James calls the law of liberty, as a mirror, we see our defects and shortcomings.

27. Who does James say will be blessed in what he does?

_____

_____

**Personal Question:** Is there an area in your life in which God has revealed your lack of obedience?

James next proceeds to discuss other aspects of obedience.

**Read James 2:10-13.**
28. If we break one point of the law we are guilty of_____

_____

29. How does James tell us to speak and act?

_____

30. Who will judgment be merciless to?

_____

31. What triumphs over judgment?

_____

Justice demands what is due her: that sinners should be condemned. Mercy pleads that they be saved.

**Discussion Question:** How can you show mercy to your neighbors this week?

**Read Matthew 6:14, 15.**
32. When will the Father not forgive your transgressions?

_____

**Discussion Question:** Why does God insist that we forgive first?

**Personal Questions:** Is there anyone you need to forgive? If there is, make sure you take the matter to God and get it worked out. What do you have to do?

Read **James 4:17.**

33.  If we know what is right to do and do not do it, to us it is _____

Read **Matthew 7:26,27.**

34.  With what does Jesus compare someone who hears His words, yet doesn't act on them?

_____

When we become a Christian, we voluntarily take upon ourselves responsibilities and obligations which ordinary persons do not acknowledge.

Read **James 1:27.**

35.  Describe pure religion (worship).

_____

_____

**Personal Questions:** How well do I measure up to this definition of pure worship? How can I improve?

**Personal Application**
1.  Keep track during the week of occasions where you fail to control yourself or to be obedient.
2.  Ask God's forgiveness and His help.
3.  Are these areas where you repeatedly fail?
4.  List what God wants you to do to overcome repeated failures.

**Memory Work**
*"But prove yourselves doers of the word, and not merely hearers who delude themselves" (Jas. 1:22).*
*"And the world is passing away, and also its lusts; but the one who does the will of God abides forever" (1 John 2:17).*

## PROVING YOURSELF IN SELF-CONTROL AND OBEDIENCE
1.  I need to learn self-control and obedience because...
2.  Anger is very displeasing to God because...
3.  By allowing God's Word to be implanted in my life I will...
4.  I truly show my obedience to God by...
5.  In my own words, true religion or worship is...

Lesson Six

# Proving Yourself in Faith and Works

## Introduction

Most Christians consider themselves neither saints nor mystics, but rather men and women who want to perform the tasks of daily life well. In this chapter James gives us guidelines, which we can apply to our moment by moment walk with the Lord, and which help us find the proper balance between faith and works.

*Prayer: Heavenly Father, help me use my faith through the deeds of kindness I share with those around me. Open my eyes to the needs of others. Help me to be Your hand extended in love to a hurting world. In Jesus' name. Amen.*

**Discussion Question:** How would you define faith? Works?

## Bible Study

Read **James 2:14-17.**
1. How does James describe faith in God unaccompanied by good works?

_____

Does James' statement surprise you? Some had claimed James had a different doctrine than Paul's "justification by faith." The difference is only in the approach of the two disciples. While James is teaching believers how to express their faith, Paul, in *Romans,* is looking at a person before he is converted. In this context, he rejects "works" as the vehicle through which salvation is received. Elsewhere, he also teaches that good works should be the Christian's response to his faith.

Read **Titus 1:16.**
2. How does Paul describe the men he is warning Titus about?

_____

_____

Read **Galatians 5:6.**
3.  What does Paul claim is of the most importance in Christ Jesus?

Read **Ephesians 2:10.**
4.  For what were we created?

Returning to James' arguments for his position now, we can almost imagine him standing before a courtroom jury, calling witnesses, giving evidence, making his case, point by point.

Read **James 2:18-20.**
5.  How does James say we can best demonstrate our faith?

**Discussion Question:** How do you think James would define "works"?

6.  Who does James give as an example of those who believe in God and yet perform no good works?

7.  What does he call the person who doesn't recognize that faith without works is useless?

8.  How does James describe faith without works in these verses?

Faith is not a creed, but a personal response to the grace of God which Jesus proclaimed. James is arguing against the idea that a confession of faith guarantees the believer's salvation regardless of his conduct.

Read **James 2:21-23.**
9.  What did Abraham do that justified him by his works?

10.  What was the relationship between his works and faith?

_____

_____


*The Living Bible* makes the meaning of the verse a little more clear: "You see, he was trusting God so much that he was willing to do whatever God told him to; his faith was made complete by what he did, by his actions, his good deeds."

Read **Hebrews 11:17-19.**
11.  What did Abraham believe God would do?

_____


Read **Genesis 22:1-14.**
12.  God did something better than raising Isaac from the dead. What did he do?

_____

13.  What did Abraham name the mountain where this event occurred?

_____


God provided a substitute sacrifice for Isaac. Yet, when the world needed a Savior, there was no substitute available for His own Son.

**Discussion Question:** Share a time when God provided in a hopeless or impossible situation.

**Personal Question:** For what kind of situation do you still lack faith that *the Lord will provide?* If you can't think of any, ask the Lord to show you.

Read **Genesis 15:6, James 2:23 and Romans 4:1-3.**
14.  Write out the scripture that is basically repeated in all these verses.

_____

_____


Read **James 2:24.**
15.  What does James say justifies a man?

**Discussion Question:** What does *justification* mean?

Read **James 2:25.**

James' next witness is Rahab the harlot?

16.  How was she justified?

 

Read **Joshua 2:1-21.**
17.  Why did Rahab hide the spies?

18.  What did she do when the spies left so the Israelites would not harm those in her home?

This red cord was a symbol of the blood of Christ and in a sense showed that salvation (in the Old Testament sense) had come to that house.

Read **Hebrews 11:31.**
19.  Why did Rahab not perish along with those who were disobedient?

In Jewish tradition Rahab has been used as the model for repentance. She was justified both by her works of hiding the spies and by her faith in accepting their God.

In one of the most striking illustrations given in the Bible, Jesus speaks to this same issue of faith and works.

Read **Matthew 25:31-46.**
This text describes a judging of nations, not of individuals. It is not the Great White Throne judgment described in Revelation, where each individual's eternal destiny is decided. However, the picture given here does show the Lord's attitude toward this aspect of "works."

20.  Who will gather before Jesus when He comes in His glory?

21. What big separation will Jesus make?

_____

_____

22. What will Jesus say to the sheep?

_____

_____

23. What was the basis of Jesus' commendation to the sheep?

_____

24. What will be their response?

_____

25. How will Jesus reply?

_____

_____

26. What does Jesus say to those on His left?

_____

_____

27. In summary, why were the nations on Jesus' left sent away?

_____

This is a very sobering thought. All of the qualities that separated those nations which received Jesus' approval and those who were sent away to eternal darkness were essentially "works." Many of us as Christians have a tendency to divide other Christians and ourselves into two groups—those who are strong in faith and those who are strong in works. Faith and works cannot be separated. Different sides of the coin, neither has worth in God's sight without the other.

**Personal Questions:** In the past have you been a "faith" only person or a "works" only person, or has your Christian life been well balanced? If the former is true, what should you do about it? Be specific.

Read **Matthew 5:16.**
28. What is the natural result of our good works?

_____

True faith in God is *naturally* accompanied by right action. Our faith shows us how much God has done for us and we automatically *want* to extend His love to others in tangible ways. Good works will never "get" us something from God. They are simply our response to His love for us.

Read **James 2:26.**
29. What is the comparison James makes to faith without works?

_____

**Personal Application**
1. List some instances where you have professed faith but lacked works to back up your profession.
2. List times when you have exercised both faith and works.
3. Write down any basic reasons you can see why you acted differently in those different situations.
4. In what areas of your life is God asking for your actions right now?
5. List specific actions.

**Memory Work**
*"For just as the body without the spirit is dead, so also faith without works is dead" (Jas. 2:26).*

## PROVING YOURSELF IN FAITH AND WORKS
1. I act out my faith in God as a response to His...
2. When I see a need and fail to act, I show that...
3. I see faith and works balance in my life by...

# Proving Yourself by Controlling Your Tongue

## Introduction

We've all heard the children's taunt, "Sticks and stones may break my bones, but words will never hurt me." But take a moment to think of your past. Do you remember the most the spankings you got or the embarrassment of a public scolding? Most of us remember the pain words have inflicted much longer than physical pain.

The tongue has been called the most dangerous part of our body, and the history of the human race proves that it's easier to tame a wild animal than to tame the tongue. Only through the power and strength of the Holy Spirit can be the tongue be brought into submission to our Lord Jesus Christ.

*Prayer: Heavenly Father, I confess that my tongue often controls me, instead of my controlling my tongue. I ask Your forgiveness and pray for strength and wisdom to speak only those things which are good, pure and edifying. In Jesus' name. Amen.*

**Personal Question:** Take a few moments to list times in the past week when you misused your tongue.

## Bible Study

Read **James 1:26.**
1. What does James say about a Christian who does not bridle his tongue?

_____

_____

We've learned by now that James is not one to mince words. This comment alone should be enough to make us keep a close check on every word that comes out of our mouth.

Read **James 3:2-5.**

2. To what two things does James compare the tongue?

_____

3. Why?

_____

_____

Read **James 3:6-12.**
4. List some of the evil aspects of the tongue.

_____

_____

_____

**Discussion Question:** The Lord, through James, has made some very serious charges. How seriously have we personally and the Christian community taken these verses?

5. According to James what two things should not come out of the same mouth?

_____

Our praise, thanks and worship to God is meaningless when we in turn curse the very thing that was made in the image of God.

6. With what does James compare blessing and cursing from the same mouth?

_____

**Discussion Question:** Why do you think James used these three particular examples?

7. Beside each of these references in Proverbs, write the evil done by the tongue.

Proverbs 10:19_____

Proverbs 17:20_____

Proverbs 18:21_____

Although we blame the tongue for what it says, at the same time we must realize that it is only an instrument.

Read **Luke 6:45.**
8.   What is the real source of the tongue's problem?

_____

Long before Jesus came, God spoke much the same idea through the lips of the prophet, Jeremiah.

Read **Jeremiah 17:9.**
9.   What did Jeremiah say about our heart?

_____

_____

**Personal Questions:** Are you willing to accept that judgment from God? Are you willing to accept the fact that your mouth spews out what is really in your heart? What does _your_ mouth indicate is in _your_ heart?

Although we cannot have a permanent change in our speaking until the Lord has had the chance to work on our heart, the opposite idea—that changing our speech pattern does change us—is in some way true as well. Let's see what some of the results are.

Read **Proverbs 21:23.**
10.   What happens when we guard our mouth and tongue?

_____

Read **James 3:1,2.**
11.   What does James tell us we are able to do if we don't stumble in what we say?

_____

12.   What does he call such a person?

_____

Read **Proverbs 15:4.**
13.   What is a soothing tongue?

_____

The Bible speaks much on how to control our tongue and how the Christian should make use of his tongue. Let's look at a few of these suggestions.

Read **Ephesians 4:31.**
14.   What does Paul tell the Ephesians to omit from their speech?

_____

_____

Read **Philippians 4:8.**
15.   Since Jesus said that the mouth speaks from the heart, what should we think on?

_____

_____

**Personal Question:** What are ten things in your life which fall in the above categories? Write them on a separate piece of paper and put it up at home where you will see it often.

Read **Ephesians 4:29.**
16.   Describe the words that should come out of our mouth.

_____

**Discussion Question:** What steps can we immediately take to improve what comes out of our mouth, thus making our words pleasing to the Lord?

Read **Luke 6:28.**
17.   What should we do if others curse us?

_____

**Personal Question:** How can I react in a more Christlike manner toward those with whom I do not get along?

Read **James 5:12.**
18.   Why does James direct us not to take an oath?

_____

In this verse James is not concerned with what we call "profanity," the reckless use of holy names to add emphasis, but with oaths taken to assure truthfulness. The danger of the use of such oaths is that men come to feel that if these are omitted, there is no binding necessity to speak the truth.

In Biblical times the Jews and Arabs were notorious for swearing or taking oaths by heaven, earth, Jerusalem, the temple, the altar and different members of the body. Even simple affirmations were accompanied with an oath. Where oaths are customary, basic honesty founded on principles is not assumed.

Read **Matthew 5:33-37.**
19. What was the ancient Israelite law concerning vows?

20. What was Jesus' command concerning oaths?

21. If our statement is more than "yes" or "no," it becomes

Read **Romans 14:11.**
22. What should every tongue do?

Read **Philippians 2:11.**
23. What does Paul tell the church in Philippi concerning what every tongue should do?

Read **Ezekiel 3:16-21.**
24. Who spoke to Ezekiel and gave him directions?

25. What was Ezekiel appointed to do?

26. If Ezekiel failed to warn the wicked people that they would die, who would be held responsible if they died?

27. If the watchmen warned the wicked and they did not change,

who would be responsible?

---

All Christians in one sense are appointed to be watchmen, to warn a wicked world of its sin against God.

Because our tongue is so difficult to control, special, divine help is available. When Jesus baptizes a Christian in the Holy Spirit, one of the largest areas of our brain, the speech center, is brought under the influence of the Holy Spirit.

Read **Acts 2:1-4.**
28. What physical manifestation accompanied the disciples' baptism in the Holy Spirit (v. 4)?

---

Speaking in tongues is the supernatural God-given ability to speak in a language which the individual has never learned. Tongues may be a known language or one that God has created just for you, a private prayer language that only He understands. We'll never understand all of God's reasons but one important reason for speaking in tongues is given in First Corinthians.

Read **1 Corinthians 14:4.**
29. What reason is given in this verse?

---

To *edify* means to *build up, confirm to strengthen.*

**Discussion Question:** Can you share a time when this has been particularly true in your life?

The Bible sometimes refers to "speaking in tongues" as *praying in the Spirit.* When we pray in the Spirit, another miracle occurs.

Read **Romans 8:26,27.**
30. How does the Holy Spirit help us?

31. Why do we need this kind of help?

Isn't this wonderful? Whenever we are unsure of what to pray, we can always pray in our prayer language and be sure we are praying in God's will.

**Personal Questions:** Are you baptized in the Holy Spirit with the outward manifestation of speaking in tongues? If not, would you like to be? (Tell your teacher.) If you are, do you use your prayer language daily to speak to God privately and, incidentally, to edify yourself?

**Personal Questions:** Go back to the list you made at the beginning of this lesson. Do you see these times of misusing your tongue as sin? Take a few moments to ask God's forgiveness if you haven't already. From whom else do you need to ask forgiveness?

### Personal Application
1. Take some time to think and pray seriously about the effect your tongue has in your life and that of others.
2. Ask God to show you specific ways to "bridle" your tongue. List them.
3. Ask God for specific ways to use your tongue to edify yourself and others. List them.
4. Make a special effort in the coming week to put these two lists into effect.

### Memory Work
*"If anyone thinks himself to be religious, and yet does not bridle his tongue but deceives his own heart, this man's religion is worthless"* (Jas. 1:26).

## PROVING YOURSELF BY CONTROLLING YOUR TONGUE
1. When my tongue is a problem, I need to realize...
2. The real source of my tongue's problem is...
3. Controlling my tongue will have the following results...
4. I need to think on...
5. I need to say...
6. The Holy Spirit helps me by...

## Lesson Eight

# Proving Yourself by Avoiding Quarrels and Conflicts

## Introduction

Jeanette and Karen attend the same church where they both sing in the choir. One morning Karen was asked to sing a solo. This made Jeanette boiling mad because she felt she had a better voice and yet she had never been asked to solo. She refused to speak to Karen. Now, Jeanette wonders why God seems so far away these days.

It is sometimes difficult for us to understand and acknowledge the reasons we are so often at odds with other Christians. Whether these conflicts occur only in our thought life or whether they are open clashes with members of our family, co-workers or fellow Christians, each conflict demonstrates our need for the love of Christ in that situation. In this lesson James gives us guidance in how to deal with the day-to-day tensions in our lives.

*Prayer: Heavenly Father, I confess I don't bring Your love into the quarrels and conflicts in my life. When things don't go my way, help me to display Your love, instead of my own anger. Teach me from Your Word how to handle quarrels and conflicts. In Jesus' name. Amen.*

**Discussion Questions:** Why do Christians disagree? Is it always wrong? What makes disagreement wrong?

## Bible Study

Read **James 4:1-3.**

1. What does James say is the source of our quarrels and conflicts?

_____

*The Living Bible* vividly translates this passage: "What is causing the quarrels and fights among you? Isn't it because there is a whole army of evil desires within you?"

2. What will we even do to satisfy these lusts (desires) within us?

Does this idea shock you? Are you convinced that you could never commit murder under any circumstances? Scripture says differently. Any desire that is not put under the control of the Holy Spirit can be stimulus for murder.

3. What is the real reason we fight and quarrel?

**Personal Question:** Think of a situation where Christians have quarreled. How would you apply James 4:1-3 to that situation?

4. When we ask, why don't we receive?

Whenever prestige, power and possessions are sought as the highest good in life, conflicts will inevitably occur. When our desires contradict our spiritual nature, we find confusion rather than bliss. Our physical vitality let loose without spiritual control only leads to destruction.

**Personal Question:** Has there been a time when your prayers weren't answered and you later learned that you had prayed with wrong motives?

Read **James 4:4.**
5. Having wrong motives is in actuality friendship with the world. What is another name for such friendship?

**Discussion Question:** Why is friendship with the world necessarily hostility toward God?

Read **Matthew 6:24.**
6. Why does Jesus tell us we cannot serve God and mammon?

Characteristics of lovers of the world are
(a) They conform to the world instead of the church.
(b) They find friends in the world instead of the church.

(c) They prefer amusements of the world.

(d) They pursue the same pleasures as the world with the same expense, extravagance and luxury.

(e) They make worldly interest the great object of living and everything else is subordinate.

**Personal Questions:** How many of the above characteristics describe you? How can you better live in the world without having friendship with the world?

Read **James 4:5,6.**
7. What does God jealously desire?

_____

This verse is easier to understand in *The Living Bible* translation: "The Holy Spirit God has placed within us watches over us with tender jealousy."

8. What does the Holy Spirit give us?

_____

**Discussion Question:** What do you think this greater grace is for?

God's greater grace is the strength to stand against all the evil desires that are warring in our flesh.

9. What is the secret to receiving God's grace?

_____

The Bible indicates that one thing God particularly hates is pride. Perhaps that is because a proud spirit is an unteachable spirit.

Read **Matthew 23:12.**
10. What does Jesus tell us about those who exalt themselves?

_____

11. What will happen to those who humble themselves?

_____

Read **James 4:7-9.**
12. To whom must our submission be?

_____

13.  How are we to respond to Satan's temptations?

_____

14.  What will happen then?

_____

The theories of Christian experience which suggest the inactivity of the human will and prescribe mere passive submission and dependence on the part of the believer are dangerous. We are taught in Scripture to draw near to God and to resist the devil. These are definite actions to be taken. First, we are told to submit to God before resisting the devil. Without complete submission to God's will, we are powerless against the devil.

**Discussion Question:** How can we better submit to God so we can resist the enemy?

15.  What commands does Jesus give?

_____

Read **1 Peter 1:22.**
16.  What is one way we can purify ourselves?

_____

Read **James 4:9,10.**
17.  Describe the mood James says we should have.

_____

**Discussion Question:** Why do you think James is prescribing such behavior?

James tells us to mourn and weep, not because Christianity is a matter of gloom and sadness but because we are tempted to miss its joy by treating our sins lightly and failing to surrender our whole heart to God.

Scripture has much to say about our practice of judging our fellow Christians, and James next addresses himself to this subject.

Read **James 4:11,12.**
18.  Why should we not speak against or judge a fellow Christian?

_____

19.  What is the one Lawgiver and Judge able to do?

_____

Read **Leviticus 19:16-18.**
20.  The Old Testament law tells us not to_____

_____

Read **James 4:13-17.**
21.  What is the sin James condemns in v. 17?

_____

Read **James 5:9.**
22.  Why should we not complain against our brethren?

_____

Read **Matthew 5:22.**
23.  James said that whoever was angry with his brother shall be

_____

_The Living Bible's_ translation of the answer is "is in danger of judgment," which is more in keeping with the thought expressed.

24.  Whoever says "you fool" shall be_____

_____

This term _fool_ was a much more serious charge than the word implies in English. It meant a wicked reprobate, destitute of all spiritual or divine knowledge.

Read **Matthew 7:1-5.**
25.  By what measure did Jesus say we would be judged?

26.  What must we first do before we remove the speck from our neighbor's eye?

_____

**Personal Questions:** Can you think of a "log" the Holy Spirit has been urging you to remove? Why don't you confess it to Him right now?

Read **Romans 14:1-4.**

27. Paul tells us to accept the one who is weak in the faith. What should we *NOT* do in regard to the weaker brother?

_____

Here Paul is speaking of the very real problem many of us have of "judging" another's Christianity, particularly the new Christian. While it is right to counsel when asked, we must be careful not to discourage her with our too-high expectations. Her growth and progress is primarily between her and the Lord.

Read **Roman 14:10-13.**

28. Who shall stand before the judgment seat of God?

_____

29. To whom must we give an account?

_____

30. Instead of judging one another, we should determine

_____

_____

Read **1 Corinthians 4:5.**

31. Paul writes that instead of passing judgment before the time we should _____

_____

_____

**Discussion Question:** How can I guard myself from judging fellow Christians?

Read **James 5:19,20.**

32. What does one do when he turns a sinner from error?

_____

Read **Romans 15:1.**

33. According to Paul, what should we who are strong do?

_____

**Discussion Question:** How do we bear the weaknesses of those who are weaker than we are?

Read **Galatians 6:1.**

34.  How should we treat a man who is caught in any trespass?

_____

35.  Why should we be gentle with the one who has sinned?

_____

Read **1 Peter 4:8.**

36.  Why does Peter tell us to keep fervent in our love for one another?

_____

The Christian must always walk the fine line between harshness and laxness or lack of caring. We can do this only through the grace of our Lord Jesus.

### Personal Application

This week I will show my love for a weaker sister or brother in the Lord by...

### Memory Work

"*Submit therefore to God. Resist the devil and he will flee from you*" *(Jas. 4:7).*

"*Above all, keep fervent in your love for one another, because love covers a multitude of sins*" *(1 Pet. 4:8).*

## PROVING YOURSELF BY AVOIDING QUARRELS AND CONFLICTS

1.  Why do we quarrel?
2.  What do our quarrels indicate about our attitude toward God?
3.  List characteristics of people who love the world.
4.  What does God provide to help us?
5.  How do we resist temptation?
6.  What attitudes should we have toward fellow Christians?